Nestor Studios • Gower and Sunset • 1913

In December of 1911, the Nestor Film Company was the first studio established in Hollywood proper and its first film was *The Law of the Range.* Located on the northwest corner of Sunset Boulevard and Gower Street in the old Blondeau Tavern (built in the 1880s), the new company started a trend of movie companies building their studio facilities in Hollywood. By 1912 there were several other film companies in Hollywood including the early Universal Studios. This trend of big companies coming from the East Coast has endured into the 21st century.

Photography: Bison Archives

To Julie!

From one "Hollywoodife"

To Another

Marc Wanamaker

2002

Hollywood

now & then

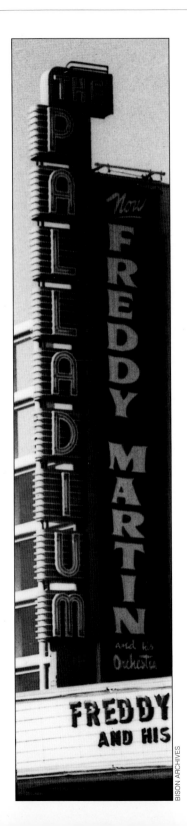

FIRST EDITION 2002
PUBLISHED BY:
GEORGE ROSS JEZEK PHOTOGRAPHY & PUBLISHING
P.O. BOX 600253
SAN DIEGO, CA 92160
(619) 582-7704

CONCEPT BY:
GEORGE ROSS JEZEK

PRODUCED BY:
GEORGE ROSS JEZEK

CONTEMPORARY PHOTOGRAPHY BY:
GEORGE ROSS JEZEK

CAPTIONS BY:
MARC WANAMAKER

BLACK & WHITE PHOTOGRAPHS PROVIDED BY:
BISON ARCHIVES
LOS ANGELES PUBLIC LIBRARY
BRUCE TORRENCE HISTORICAL COLLECTION
DINO AND GREG WILLIAMS COLLECTION

ALL COLOR PHOTOGRAPHS © GEORGE ROSS JEZEK

ISBN 0-9701036-1-1

GRAPHIC DESIGN BY:
MINK GRAPHIC DESIGN

PRINTED IN HONG KONG THROUGH CREATIVE PRINT MANAGEMENT, USA

BISON ARCHIVES

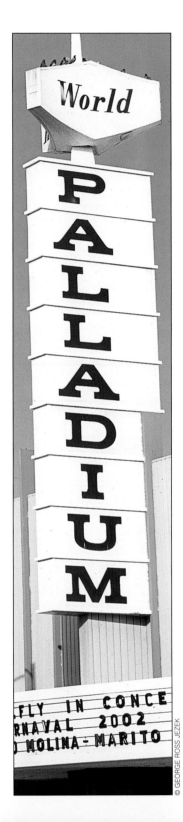

© GEORGE ROSS JEZEK

This book is dedicated to my parents who always encouraged me and

believed in my passion for photography.

G.R.J.

Table of Contents

Introduction BY JOHNNY GRANT

Hollywood is a community that has a storied history worth preserving. It appears that almost everybody in the world develops and emotional tie to Tinseltown when they get their first glimpse of those larger-than-life, moving images on the silver screen.

I hope that we'll take lessons from those early-day showmen and hype-meisters and duplicate the manufactured glamour and events that excited so many, so long ago, on Hollywood Boulevard.

A glamorous example of recent Tinseltown hype took place when Hollywood Boulevard was ceremoniously re-named (for a 24-hour period) Elizabeth Taylor Way as a publicity vehicle to draw attention to a television special honoring the superstar. Seventeen "Boulevard" signs were placed in the designated area for the name-change with media from around the world covering the event. Other manufactured glamour includes world premieres, celebrity parades, walk of fame hand and footprint ceremonies.

Established as its own city on November 14, 1903, Hollywood was governed by a board of five trustees. In 1910, it was decided to connect with the City of Los Angeles when a water shortage became a tremendous problem and annexing offered them a plentiful supply. The last action taken by that board was to rename Prospect Avenue to the world-famous "Hollywood Boulevard."

In prehistoric times the hills, behind where the Hollywood Bowl is now located, served as home to saber tooth tigers and mammoth bison. Later George Allen, known as Greek George, brought a drove of camels to the area. The animals were originally to be used by the United States Army for desert transportation. When that proved unsuccessful, Greek George turned them loose in the hills, where they roamed at will, occasionally to be caught and raced against horses in the fiestas of downtown Los Angeles.

In the early days of motion pictures, there were no studio commissaries. Actors and extras often walked to get lunch and you could see a costumed Abraham Lincoln or General Ulysses S. Grant, along with priests and ladies of the evening, side by side, strolling the Boulevard.

At this time, when pictures first began, circus people and sideshow attractions alike came to Hollywood looking for work. The streets were colorful and became known as "walking Vaudeville," and when the cowboys began hanging out at Sunset at Gower, that area was dubbed "Gower Gulch."

In those early days, one thousand dollars would have bought the Broadway Department Store location at Hollywood and Vine.

Our community has been revitalized with the recent Hollywood and Highland project, many new stores, restaurants and nightclubs. The little man in the gold suit, Oscar, was the spark plug of our revivification program with his elegant new home the Kodak Theatre located in the Hollywood and Highland project. At the same location, the near replica of D.W. Griffith's "Intolerance" set has proven to be a very popular attraction with tourists from around the world and a site for studio media events, drawing many famous faces.

Hollywood Now & Then brings back a multitude of great memories for me as I look at the photographs of Hollywood sites, past and present. It is gratifying to see the old intersection of Hollywood and Vine (which was originally a grape vineyard), now in a transformation that will reemphasize its historical significance.

I can almost see Sid Grauman standing in front of his luxurious movie emporium, talking with tourists at the remodeled Grauman's Chinese Theatre. I hope you enjoy this visual tour of remarkable and noteworthy images. It is a valuable collection for anyone interested in Hollywood's past, present and future.

Hooray for Hollywood!

Johnny Grant

Mr. Johnny Grant is the honorary Mayor of Hollywood. He has also been the Chairman of the Hollywood Walk of Fame committee, since 1980.

The A.G. Bartlett mansion rests on a knoll above Hollywood Boulevard near Argyle Avenue. The Bartlett estate was one of several large farms specializing in citrus farming, the dominant business in turn-of-the-century Hollywood. The mission-style house became a tourist attraction mentioned in several promotional brochures as early as 1905. When Jose Mascarel opened his Vista del Mar tract in 1901, A.G. Bartlett, a Los Angeles sheet music publisher, purchased seven acres north of Prospect Avenue (later Hollywood Boulevard) at Argyle Avenue. Bartlett built a large home on the summit of the property and lived there until his death in 1923. The house had 15,000 square feet of space and was one of the finest of the era. The house featured a reception room, library, and for his daughter an opera singer, a music hall that seated 250 guests.

The Bartlett Foothills of Hollywood above Argyle and Yucca Streets were subdivided in the 1920s resulting in a mixture of apartment houses, single-family homes and office buildings. On the east side of Argyle, nestled among trees that remain from the original Bartlett estate, is the Country Church of Hollywood, built as a radio broadcasting church in 1932. On the west side of Argyle is KFWB radio which moved there in the 1970s, continuing the street's radio tradition.

BISON ARCHIVES

Beachwood Valley, as seen in this photograph, was a citrus farm with groves of trees filling the entire area. The main house of the Henry Claussen Farm was situated on a hill overlooking a dirt road that is now Beachwood Drive. With beautiful views to the north, south and east, surrounding the two-story structure was a galleried patio. Located at 6116 Winans Drive, near the corner of Beachwood, the house was built around 1880 and is one of the oldest Hollywood houses that still exists today as an apartment house.

It took a century to fill in the vast citrus groves to create the Beachwood Valley of today. Beachwood Drive, north Gower Street and Winans Drive are all lost in this view, covered with trees and houses that dominate the once open valley. Now Beachwood Valley is the entrance to what was the Hollywoodland development of 1923. The sign that originally advertised the area was eventually shortened to read "Hollywood" and has become renowned as "The Hollywood Sign." The majority of the houses in this valley and in the Hollywood Hills are of Spanish Mediterranean architecture, the dominant style of Southern California residences throughout the 1920s, '30s and '40s.

The world famous Beverly Hills hotel at Crescent Drive and Sunset Boulevard is still considered one of the finest hotels in the world. Built in 1912, before Beverly Hills was incorporated as a city, the resort hotel was intended to lure prospective real estate investors to Beverly Hills. The Anderson family from the Hollywood Hotel was brought in to build and operate the new hotel. The result was not only a beautiful inn, but also a cultural and civic center. The new Beverly Hills Hotel featured the area's first movie theater and was the site of the city's first municipal election. The hotel served as a meeting place for the rich and famous, such as King Gillette, Will Rogers and Gloria Swanson along with many foreign visitors.

The "Pink Palace" as it has been called for decades, still is the center of social activity within the city of Beverly Hills. With its dominant position on a hill at Sunset Boulevard, Rodeo and Crescent Drives, the legendary hotel which was remodeled in the 1990s, is a popular venue for many social events. Its Polo Lounge is still a hangout for Hollywood dealmakers and stars, much as it was in its earliest days. Celebrities such as Howard Hughes, Lana Turner, Marilyn Monroe and others frequented the hotel over the years making it world famous. The rich and famous still frequent the Beverly Hills Hotel to this day.

BISON ARCHIVES

The first thing one sees in this aerial photograph of Beverly Hills is a colossal speedway dominating the area. The speedway a wooden track was moved from Culver City to Beverly Hills in 1921 in order to attract attention from real estate interests to the city of Beverly Hills. The site of horse and dog shows, as well as car races, the track was located on Wilshire Boulevard between Beverly Drive on the east and Lasky Drive to the west, and was the largest of its kind. By 1924, the track was removed making way for further real estate development in the area.

The "business triangle," as it is called today, stretches along South Santa Monica Boulevard to the north and Wilshire Boulevard to the south. Neiman Marcus, Saks Fifth Avenue and Barney's all have large emporia along this stretch of Wilshire Boulevard. The business triangle incorporates such sites as the Beverly Wilshire Hotel, theaters, restaurants and other attractions that have made this city-within-a-city an internationally known tourist destination.

A Santa Monica-bound streetcar on Hollywood Boulevard (which was named Prospect Avenue in 1908) is seen crossing Cahuenga Boulevard on a beautiful summer's day. Hollywood at the turn of the century was a rural area with pepper-tree-lined dirt streets and magnificent Victorian-style homes. The wealthy Midwesterners who had winter homes in California considered Hollywood to be a resort town. Although it had been incorporated as a city in 1903, Hollywood gave up its citihood a few years later to become part of Los Angeles.

The same view of Cahuenga and Hollywood Boulevards (with a city bus crossing Cahuenga) points out the dramatic changes in Hollywood in one hundred years. Transformed from a residential area into a modern city, one of the world's most famous city still has the same sense of being the small town that it had centuries ago. It was here, at Hollywood Boulevard and Cahuenga, where many motion pictures were filmed over the years.

In the early 1900s Cahuenga Pass was the most important road between the San Fernando Valley and Hollywood. For many years there was only one dirt road through the pass. In 1913 a streetcar line was built that connected the Valley with Hollywood. By the 1920s a paved road was built and after World War II a modern freeway system took over.

The Cahuenga Pass entrance today has several roads leading into the Pass: Wilcox, Highland and Franklin Avenues. From the north, Barham, Cahuenga and Lankershim Boulevards lead into Hollywood linking several communities just as they did in the 19th century. The pass has become one of the busiest arteries of north/south traffic in Southern California.

LOS ANGELES PUBLIC LIBRARY

As late as 1922, the Cahuenga Pass was still a rural area with its small canyon communities nestled in the pass, making it a country haven literally minutes from the built-up Hollywood to the south. By this time there were two tracks for the streetcar and freight rail lines that transversed the pass into North Hollywood. The road was still a two-lane winding ribbon that became more and more heavily used, causing early traffic jams. A dry creek, between the rail line and the road, is now under the freeway.

It was the Gabrieleno Indians of the Hollywood Hills who named the pass Cahuengna, meaning "little hills." The Spanish simplified the name to *Cahuenga* and after Los Angeles became a pueblo in 1781. The pass became a branch of the *El Camino Real del Rey*, the principal north/south passageway along the coast. Cahuenga Pass was filled in with a new freeway built in 1954 that is now known as the Hollywood Freeway one of the most heavily traveled freeways in southern California.

Castillo del Lago was designed by John DeLario, one of the many important architects who designed homes in the Hollywoodland development in the 1920s. DeLario had already become known for his Spanish Colonial Revival architectural style when oil explorer Patrick Logan noticed him. Logan commissioned the architect to create a castle in the hills of Hollywoodland that would stand out like no other. Castillo del Lago took $250,000 and three years to build with its nine levels up the hill. In 1926, the finished mansion had 20,000 square feet with 12,000 square feet taken up by winding staircases and towers.

Now a successful neighborhood, the old Hollywoodland is still crowned with Castillo del Lago, a landmark because of its famous and infamous tenants. In the 1930s, gangster Bugsey Siegel ran a speakeasy and gambling den there. By 1953 the estate lay empty and had various owners until pop singer Madonna purchased the castle in the 1990s and painted it reddish-brown with white stripes. Today trees and hedges obscure the grandeur of Castillo del Lago, but it still is one of Hollywood's most legendary estates.

On the site of the first motion picture studio in Hollywood, Columbia Broadcasting System built its $2 million facility, *Columbia Square*, at the northwest corner of Gower and Sunset.
At the opening day ceremony in 1938, Hollywood columnist Hedda Hopper held her broadcast there with many famed film and radio stars as her guests.
At this time CBS established KNX, its West Coast radio station, which still is in operation.

CBS purchased the Sunset-Gower property in 1937 and demolished the old wooden structures that were once the Nestor-Christie studios. Designed by architect William Lescaze, *Columbia Square* housed six studios and staff executive offices. Two of the studios were two stories high and seated 100 people. Many of the major CBS coast-to-coast shows originated there including the first pilot of the *I Love Lucy Show*. Later the two-story structure next to it housed CBS management, CBS Artists' Bureau, a branch of the Bank of America and a popular hangout, Radio Center Restaurant. Not much has changed today however; CBS still operates the facility as its CBS News headquarters, where a daily broadcast is still ongoing since the 1950s.

BISON ARCHIVES

In 1917 Charles Chaplin purchased the R.S. McClellan estate on the south-east corner of Sunset Boulevard and La Brea Avenue. By March of 1918, Chaplin opened his new studio at 1416 N. La Brea Avenue. The buildings were designed as English country style cottages with a Tudor-style gate. Before the year was finished he completed his first film at the new studio entitled, *A Dog's Life.* With the coming of 1919 United Artists was born and for the next thirty years he produced his own films there, including *The Kid, The Gold Rush, Modern Times, The Great Dictator* and *Limelight.* Not only did the studio become a Hollywood landmark it also became Chaplin's "home away from home" where he entertained world-class celebrities when they came to Los Angeles.

Between June and July of 1929, all the buildings on La Brea Avenue were moved back 15-feet for street widening. At this time Chaplin enclosed his old open stage and built another adjacent to it. After Charles Chaplin left the United States in 1953, never to return, the studio was sold to the Kling Company of Chicago and later to Red Skelton. The studio in the 1950s hosted such TV shows as, *Superman, Perry Mason,* and American International Pictures. By 1966 the lot was purchased by Herb and Dave Alpert and their record label, A&M Records. With the coming of the new Millennium, the studio was purchased by the Jim Henson Company, the producers of *The Muppets,* as its headquarters. Today Kermit the Frog, dressed as "The Tramp", waves his Chaplin derby hat to thousands of automobiles passing by this famed landmark of Hollywood.

LOS ANGELES PUBLIC LIBRARY

The Chaplin Studio on La Brea Avenue has always been a tourist attraction in Hollywood since it was built in 1918. Some of Chaplin's films made there included, *The Kid, A Woman of Paris, The Circus, City Lights, Modern Times* and *Limelight.* Between January and February of 1939 Chaplin soundproofed his stages for 'sound' film production along with other facilities on his small studio lot. In the 1970s the studio was designated a National Landmark noting its unusual architecture and cultural landmark status.

La Brea Avenue today is a major thoroughfare in Hollywood leading to Hollywood Boulevard and the Cahuenga Pass. Over the years the studio was used as a location by many companies producing television shows and motion pictures. During the 1950s Universal shot several feature films on the lot, one of them entitled, *Hollywood Story.* The studio was used in 1992 as a backdrop location for the motion picture, *Chaplin.* Robert Downey Jr., starring as Chaplin, stops in front of the studio to take one last look before leaving Hollywood forever after he had been in town to receive his Special Academy Award.

At the southeast corner of Melrose and Bronson Avenues, in the midst of open fields, were the Clune Studios. Originally this farm was the site of the Fiction Players Studios, established there in 1915, and was later purchased by Famous Players Company of New York shortly thereafter. Famous Players' star Mary Pickford shot one of her early California films there, *A Girl from Yesterday*. Later, when the studio was sold to theater magnate William H. Clune, it became a rental studio used for independent films. By 1919, after the formation of United Artists Pictures, famed silent film star Douglas Fairbanks made Clune Studios his headquarters. There he made *The Mark of Zorro* (1920) and *The Three Musketeers* (1921), but by 1922, he left the lot to buy another studio nearby, where United Artists would flourish for the next three decades.

Raleigh Studios, which was always owned by William H. Clune, changed names over the years. It became known as the Douglas Fairbanks Studios, Clune Studios, Tec Art Studios, Inspiration, Prudential, California, Producers and in 1990, Raleigh. Before Paramount Studios took over the north side of Melrose Avenue, there had been several studios there, as well. When Clune operated his lot on the south side of Melrose from 1915 to 1926, the site of what is now Paramount was his backlot. Feature films, shorts, commercials, television shows and music videos have all been made on the Raleigh lot. From the first *Superman* pilot for television and *Gunsmoke,* to films featuring stars whose careers spanned the decades such as Charles Chaplin, Doug Fairbanks, Ingrid Bergman and Frank Sinatra, the studio has seen the history of Hollywood pass through its gates.

In 1938, near the southeast corner of Sunset and Gower, many small independent studios stood since the early part of the century. The first silent film studio was established in the vicinity in 1911. By 1926 the neighborhood became the home of Columbia Studios at 1438 North Gower Street. There, many of the Columbia classic films were shot, including *Lost Horizon* with Ronald Colman, *It Happened One Night* with Clark Gable and Claudette Colbert, *Gilda* with Rita Hayworth and *The Three Stooges* shorts. During the 1960s, Colgems television produced shows there such as *The Monkees*.

In 1972, Columbia Studios moved across the Hollywood Hills to Burbank where it entered into a facilities-sharing agreement with Warner Studios. Columbia remained there for twenty years until moving to its present site at the old MGM Studios in Culver City, now Sony. The Hollywood facility was taken over by a rental company and renamed, *Sunset Gower Independent Studios*, where they improved the studio lot. Shortly thereafter they leased the studio to such legendary television show productions as *General Hospital* and *Days of Our Lives*, as well as many feature films, television shows and commercial producers. In the 1970s a sampling of shows taped there included: *The Kraft Anniversary Show, Donny and Marie Show, Sonny and Cher Show,* and in the 1980s and 90s, *Benson* and *Married with Children. The China Syndrome* starring Michael Douglas, as well as other feature films throughout the '70s, '80s and '90s, used the Sunset-Gower Studios as their primary facility.

Theater impresario Sid Grauman opened his Egyptian Theater in 1922 on Hollywood Boulevard with the gala premiere of *Robin Hood* starring his friend Douglas Fairbanks. The Egyptian was the first movie palace built in Hollywood. Its architects, Meyer and Holler, were the first to capitalize on the Egyptian craze as a style for theaters shortly after the discovery of King Tut's tomb in Egypt at this time. The Egyptian Theater was the first theater to host a premiere in Hollywood, which led to the tradition that has become commonplace.

Like the old Grauman's Chinese Theater, the Egyptian is characterized by a large forecourt fronting Hollywood Boulevard, which was originally surrounded with Middle Eastern shops, flanked by guards in ancient Egyptian costumes. There, in 1923 Cecil B. DeMille premiered his most famous film, *The Ten Commandments,* with thousands in attendance to glimpse at their favorite stars. Inside the theater, restored in the 1990s by the American Cinematheque, hieroglyphic murals, a sunburst ceiling and a giant scarab above the proscenium continued the Egyptian theme. Thanks to the American Cinematheque, the theater has been given back to the community and it remains a significant Hollywood landmark.

In 1926 C. E. Toberman, Hollywood's premiere builder, opened a lavish legitimate theater on Hollywood Boulevard, across the street from the Grauman's Chinese Theater. Called the El Capitan, the theater featured an opulent East Indian interior, the creation of architect G. Albert Lansburgh. The theater was housed in a multi-story office building with an intricately carved facade decorated with characters from literature and drama. The first production at the El Capitan was a British revue called, *Charlot's Revue of 1924* starring Beatrice Lillie, Gertrude Lawrence and Jack Buchanan.

LOS ANGELES PUBLIC LIBRARY

© GEORGE ROSS JEZEK

In 1941, the El Capitan was converted temporarily into a movie theater for the premiere and run of Orson Welles' *Citizen Kane.* By 1942 Paramount renovated and permanently converted the El Capitan into a film theater renaming it the Paramount Theater. The first film to premiere at the new Paramount was Cecil B. DeMille's *Reap The Wild Wind* starring John Wayne. After many years of different owners and renovations, the theater was renamed the *El Capitan* in 1985, when the Disney Company assumed a long-term lease on the property and totally restored the theater to its former glory in the 1990s.

BISON ARCHIVES

This unique photograph of the backlot of Fine Arts Studios shows the world famous *Intolerance* sets of film director D. W. Griffith as they stood at the corner of Hillhurst Avenue, Sunset and Hollywood Boulevards in 1917. Today *Intolerance*, made in 1916, is a symbol of Hollywood's silent film era. This backlot was also the site of sets for Griffith's epic Civil War film, *The Birth Of A Nation*, made in 1915. The *Intolerance* sets, standing over 150 feet high, became an international tourist attraction until they were torn down in 1920. The old Fine Arts Studio was originally located on the southwest corner of Virgil Avenue and Sunset Boulevard, which became a part of a historic studio district since many of Hollywood's earliest studios were built nearby.

The Vista Theater, which stands at the intersection of Hillhurst Avenue, Sunset and Hollywood Boulevards, opened in 1923 as the Hollywood Bard Theater. The first premiere at the theater was *Captain January*. This neighborhood theater in east Hollywood has been in continuous operation since then, and was remodeled with an Egyptian motif inside, making it a novelty among theaters in modern Los Angeles. Many of the original studios in the neighborhood are still operating as film and television studios such as KCET-TV, ABC-TV Center, and Triangle Studios.

On the site of the Burbank family ranch at the intersection of Olive Avenue and Barham Boulevard, the First National Pictures Corporation built its state-of-the-art studio in 1926. The property was open farmland in the midst of the San Fernando Valley, the ideal location for a motion picture studio. First National was established in New York in 1918, and with the advent of sound pictures began to prepare for the sound revolution by building a west coast studio that could handle the new sound film technology. By 1928 Warner Brothers Pictures purchased the assets of First National and took over the studio renaming it Warner Bros.-First National Studios.

For more than 70 years, the Warner Bros. Studios in Burbank has been one of Los Angeles' most historic motion picture studios, the place where many American classic films were produced. Films such as *Casablanca* with Humphrey Bogart to *My Fair Lady* starring Audrey Hepburn were made at the Burbank lot. Famous Warner television shows such as *Maverick*, *77 Sunset Strip* and in more recent times, *ER* and *Buffy The Vampire Slayer* were also made there. The studio with its many sound stages and extensive backlot settings continues to be one of the largest studio lots in the world.

Built by Hollywood developer Charles E. Toberman for theater magnate Sid Grauman in 1927, the Chinese Theater is the most famous movie house in the world. The theater became a symbol of Hollywood and the motion picture industry when it opened its doors with the first of its many film premieres, Cecil B. DeMille's *The King of Kings.* As seen in this photo, *Hell's Angels,* a Howard Hughes production starring Jean Harlow, premiered in 1930. The hand and footprints of Hollywood stars that are embedded in the cement of its forecourt and the ceremonies that surrounded the creation of each have made the theater a legend in its own right. The tradition began when Sid Grauman was showing off the newly constructed theater to his friends and investors Douglas Fairbanks, Mary Pickford and Norma Talmadge. They stepped onto the sidewalk and left faint footprints in the wet cement. Grauman celebrated the mistake, garnering publicity that has long outlived him.

At the beginning of 2002, the Chinese Theater was restored and reopened as Grauman's Chinese Theater, true to its Hollywood legacy. The theater is still one of the most famous Hollywood landmarks, where many film premieres and the Academy Awards were held in 1944, 1945 and 1946. New stars and films continue to be seen at the theater with the latest premiere of *Star Wars: Episode II-Attack of the Clones*, which opened in the summer of 2002. The Chinese Theater has always been a treasure of movie theater architecture and interior design, a Chinese-Japanese-Art Deco motif, which has become a symbol of Hollywood past and present.

LOS ANGELES PUBLIC LIBRARY

In 1930 the Los Angeles City Board of Park Commissioners decided that it would make use of the trust fund that Colonel Griffith J. Griffith had willed to the city (a gift which also included the entirety of Griffith Park) when he died in 1919. He had called for a Greek Theater, an observatory and a hall of science to be built on Mount Hollywood.
When the Greek Theater was completed in September of 1930 it became one of Hollywood's most popular musical venues. The Greek Theater, also known for having the architectural distinction of a simple Doric design, has outdoor seating for 4,500.

Since 1946 with its first season of outdoor light opera and musical comedy, the Greek Theater has been the venue of countless music, theater, dance and multi-media performances. Nestled in the foothills of Griffith Park, the theater has been a showplace for such performers as Spanish dancer, Jose Greco in the 1960s, and singers Joni Mitchell and Crosby, Stills, Nash and Young in the 1970s. In more recent times, The Gypsy Kings, Alanis Morissette, Jackson Browne and many others frequently played there. The Greek continues to be one of the most unique theatrical venues and architectural novelties in Los Angeles and has a continuing schedule of a broad mixture of music for a diverse Los Angeles audience.

In 1902 Highland Avenue was one of the main thoroughfares into the mouth of Cahuenga Pass. At Highland and Propect Avenues (now Hollywood Boulevard) the Hollywood Hotel was built in 1903 as a gateway to the north. Adjacent to Highland and Franklin Avenue on the H.J. Whitley property is Whitley Heights, a residential development at the time, and a gateway to the Pass. In 1910, the first dramatic filmmaking took place when D.W. Griffith filmed *In Old California* in and around the mouth of Cahuenga Pass. Between 1914 and 1916, director Cecil B. DeMille and his brother William lived in the neighborhood in large craftsman-style homes. DeMille said that he would sometimes ride his horse from his home to work at the Lasky Studios at the corner of Selma Avenue and Vine Street about two miles away.

North Highland Avenue is a major artery to the Cahuenga Pass that leads directly to the Hollywood Freeway. One of the most highly traveled streets in Hollywood serving thousands of cars per hour, the street is home to the famed Hollywood Bowl. Located across from the Bowl is the Hollywood Heritage Museum housed in the old Lasky-DeMille barn/studio, where Cecil B. DeMille directed Hollywood's first dramatic feature film in late 1913. The pass also is the home of the Hollywood Legion building and the old Pilgrimage Theater, where drama and music is performed during the summer months.

Beachwood Canyon became famous when developers began to advertise their new residential development called Hollywoodland. Until 1923, when the upper canyon was being prepared for home sites, the area was rural and wild; indeed, people often went hunting and camping in the wilderness. Located north of Franklin Avenue and one canyon east of the Cahuenga Pass, this area is considered one of Hollywood's important historic districts, and continues as a popular place to live for those who want to experience a bit of 'old' Hollywood.

Beachwood Canyon is situated near the Hollywood Freeway, not far from the San Fernando Valley and Downtown Los Angeles. Hollywood stretches below Beachwood Canyon making the Hollywood Hills a popular and convenient place to live, but still maintains the feel of the country. Beachwood Canyon was originally a village site for the Gabrieleno Indians, the original inhabitants of the area. Feature films were made in Beachwood Canyon, including *The Invasion of the Body Snatchers* that used the Hollywoodland Village as a small town setting in 1956. The Canyon Market and Cafe are popular meeting places not only for Hollywoodland residents but for entertainment industry people, as well.

Hollywood Boulevard and Hollywood are world famous due to continuous promotion and marketing since the turn of the 20th century. As early as 1905, the Hollywood area was a destination for the tourists, where there were tour buses taking people around the citrus groves and showing the area, all with the intent to promote real estate sales. Photographs such as this one were used in the 1920s to lure people to the glamorous "street of the stars." With the Chinese Theater, El Capitan Theater and the Hollywood Hotel all within walking distance of each other, Hollywood of 1929 had many of the same buildings that distinguish it today.

Grauman's Chinese Theater, the El Capitan Theater and the Hollywood Roosevelt Hotel remain, and promotion and marketing are still the norm in Hollywood. As seen in this photograph Hollywood Boulevard is closed for a grand premier. The newest tourist attraction is the theater and shopping complex on the corner of Highland and Hollywood Boulevards creating new life for the area on the original site of the Hollywood Hotel. There, major motion pictures will make their debuts and every year the Academy Awards will be held in the Kodak Theater, a huge facility created to protect and preserve the traditions of Hollywood. It is fitting that it sits at a corner that has been called "The Gateway to Hollywood."

The south side of Hollywood Boulevard at Cahuenga was the center of civic life in Hollywood around 1911. Dr. Palmer, who had owned the property, developed the south side of the boulevard into a mini civic center. On the southeast corner was the old City Hall (replaced by Wilcox Hall), and on the southwest corner was the Creque Bank building and a small social center, Toberman Hall. As early as 1915, filmmakers such as Buster Keaton were using these buildings and the streets and alleys nearby for real-life settings for their films.

Streetcars were available at all times on the boulevard until the late 1950s when they were replaced by a bus system.

In 1933, the corner of Hollywood Boulevard and Cahuenga was re-developed when the Creque Building expanded with two more stories, and its exterior was refaced with decorative brick. The former Hollywood City Hall and Fire Department were removed, and by 1934 Wilcox Hall was demolished for a streamline Moderne-style medical building named the Julian Medical Building. The Beveridge family (Daeida Wilcox Beveridge built Wilcox Hall) financed the project that changed the intersection dramatically. On the southeast corner is World Book and News, Hollywood's oldest newsstand that is still one of the largest in the Los Angeles area.

Prospect Avenue (later known as Hollywood Boulevard) east of Gower Street was quite devoid of trees, so the boulevard's homes looked naked as they sat side by side on open fields. The estates on the Avenue were built for the most part by wealthy Midwesterners who came to Southern California during the winter months. It wasn't until 1903 that Hollywood became a city in its own right. The new city began to take shape as a viable community with businesses and services with its new Hollywood Hotel as its cultural center. In this early photograph one can see the streetcar that connected downtown Los Angeles with Hollywood and other communities to the west. The house of Hollywood's first mayor, Sanford Rich, is on the far right with its signature observation tower.

To the east from Gower Street, Hollywood Boulevard stretches all the way to the East Hollywood Hills. Once streetcars made their way from Downtown Los Angeles into East Hollywood, past the old film studios and west to Hollywood Boulevard and into West Hollywood and Beverly Hills. Further east on the north side of the street stood the Hawaii Theater and the Florentine Gardens, the latter is still in operation as a dance club. Just west of Hollywood Boulevard and Gower Street is the famed Henry Fonda Theater that was once known as the Music Box, built in 1926.

The Christie Hotel had become a landmark on the Boulevard when it was built in 1923 at McCadden Place. C.E. Toberman, and Al and Charles Christie erected the hotel claiming it was the newest luxury hotel on the Boulevard. Al Christie, an important studio mogul, said that the building was Hollywood's second tallest skyscraper, even though it was only six stories high. The Greenwich Village Cafe opened in the basement and later became the New Yorker Club. Its proximity to the new Egyptian Theater helped make the Christie Hotel a popular destination.

The old Christie Hotel at McCadden Place has changed hands over the years and now belongs to the Church of Scientology. The imposing building, a landmark on the Boulevard for almost 80 years, continues to be recognized as one of Hollywood's historic architectural sites. Next door, the Egyptian Theater was carefully remodeled in the '90s by the American Cinematheque and remains a Hollywood landmark along with a replica Pig 'n' Whistle restaurant-bar that once was popular on the boulevard in the 1930s and '40s.

Located one block east of Ivar on the northeast corner of Hollywood Boulevard and Cahuenga, the old Security Trust and Savings Bank Building was Hollywood's first six-story skyscraper. Thousands attended a huge celebration surrounding its June 3, 1922 opening. An orchestra played in the lobby and 3,000 souvenir booklets entitled *In The Valley of the Cahuengas* were given to guests. The intersection still has a sense of history due to many of the original buildings that still exist.

The Ivar Avenue neighborhood has been reborn with the renovation of the Security Bank Building on the northeast corner of Hollywood and Cahuenga. The renovation of several businesses on each corner of Hollywood and Ivar, as well as the street improvements south on Ivar have been in progress during the last two decades. North on Ivar, the old Knickerbocker Hotel has become a retirement home. Both north and south on Ivar, new life has come to several of its office buildings.

It had been two years since Hollywood became a city when this photograph was taken from the hills overlooking Orchid Avenue and Orange Drive. The population of the area was only 700.
In the foreground, on Orange Drive, a mission-style mansion was the home of silent screen star Conway Tearle, and in 1936 became the home of the Society of American Cinematographers.
On the right, at the end of Orange Drive, stands a large home that is the current site of the Hollywood Roosevelt Hotel. In the upper center of the photograph is
Hollywood High School, and to the far left is the Hollywood Hotel with old Prospect Avenue (now Hollywood Boulevard) directly between.

The buildings and trees of modern day Hollywood obliterate much of the old Hollywood that might have been seen from high above on Yamashiro Hill. To the left is the newly renovated Hollywood Renaissance Hotel at the Hollywood and Highland complex, and to the right is the Hollywood Roosevelt Hotel on the Boulevard. Throughout its history, Hollywood Boulevard has been on a roller coaster of booms and busts, but with its current rebirth, a boom of historic preservation seems to be cause for an economic boom as well.

Hollywood Boulevard was graced with a new luxury hotel with the opening of the Hollywood Roosevelt in 1927. As seen from this vantage point at Sycamore Avenue and looking west, the hotel stands out as one of Hollywood's most famous landmarks. Built with United Artists Studio money, the Roosevelt and its neighbor Grauman's Chinese Theater (which was built the same year), caused a Boulevard boom at the end of the 1920s. With the coming of the 1930s, the Roosevelt Hotel became the first home of the Academy Of Motion Picture Arts and Sciences and its first awards ceremony.

The Hollywood Roosevelt has been under a renovation and restoration program that began in 2002, one of many new programs dedicated to renewing an aging Hollywood. The opening of the new Hollywood and Highland project across the street and the newly renovated Grauman's Chinese Theater has helped rejuvenate the West end of Hollywood Boulevard. This historic district has gone through many changes over the years, but with the restored El Capitan Theater and other development projects in the vicinity, a new Hollywood is on the horizon.

In 1936, the intersection of Hollywood and Highland Avenue was one of the most important spots in the social and economic life of Hollywood. The Hollywood Hotel opened in 1903, the Chinese Theater opened in 1927, and the First National Bank Tower in 1928. The Hollywood Hotel was the center of Hollywood's social life until the 1950s when the hotel was closed and demolished (1956) ending an historic era.

The new Hollywood and Highland complex incorporates the Kodak Theater, new home to the annual Academy Awards presentations. The first Academy Awards event held in the new venue was in March of 2002 bringing back a sense of the golden years of Hollywood's past. The central motif of the new project incorporates two elephant columns and a Babylonian temple wall, all inspired from the settings of D.W. Griffith's 1916 feature film, *Intolerance*.

Prospect Avenue, later known as Hollywood Boulevard, was a country road passing through tracts of citrus orchards and open fields in the 19th century. In 1898 the dirt road passing through Hollywood was graded by a steam engine preparing the area for city hood in 1903. The old streets of Hollywood were predominately lined with pepper trees for over forty years before being replaced with palm trees in the 1950s.

By 1910, one house after another was developed into commercial buildings. In 1987 the last Victorian house on the boulevard was restored and became a Hollywood visitors center. By 1915 many stores were built on the Boulevard, and by the 1930s high-end shops were dominating the business community.

LOS ANGELES PUBLIC LIBRARY

The Hollywood Bowl is one of the most famous Hollywood landmarks in the world. Known as the home of "Symphonies Under the Stars," the Bowl has always been the site of Easter Services even before the shell was built. Owned by the City of Los Angeles and operated by the Hollywood Bowl Association, it is acknowledged as one of the largest natural amphitheater in the world. The Bowl site was purchased in 1919 and the first concert was held there on July 11, 1922. In 1926 Myron Hunt, who also designed Pasadena's Rose Bowl, designed the seating area that embraces the hills. Architect Lloyd Wright, the eldest son of Frank Lloyd Wright, designed the first two shells in 1927 and 1928.

The Hollywood Bowl continues to be the premiere summer venue for a diverse array of entertainment programs. The Bowl has featured most of the world's important and famous performers on its stage, from great classical musicians and orchestras to the biggest names in pop, from Jascha Heifetz and Benny Goodman to Frank Sinatra and the Beatles. Over the years there has been a succession of four shells culminating in the 1929 shell, which presently remains. With its latest acoustical improvements designed by architect Frank Gehry in 1980, the Bowl continues to be the summer home of the Los Angeles Philharmonic and the Hollywood Bowl Orchestra.

In this revealing photograph of the Hollywood Dam devoid of vegetation, the Hollywood Hills hide Lake Hollywood. In the center of the photograph is the Hollywood Professional Building built in 1929, designed by architect H.L. Goyerty. The Art Deco-style office building, intended to provide space for agents and producers, was a part of the development of Hollywood that was underway before the stock market crash of 1929. In the early 1940s, *Variety* offices were located on the ground floor, along with a restaurant, barbershop and printing company.

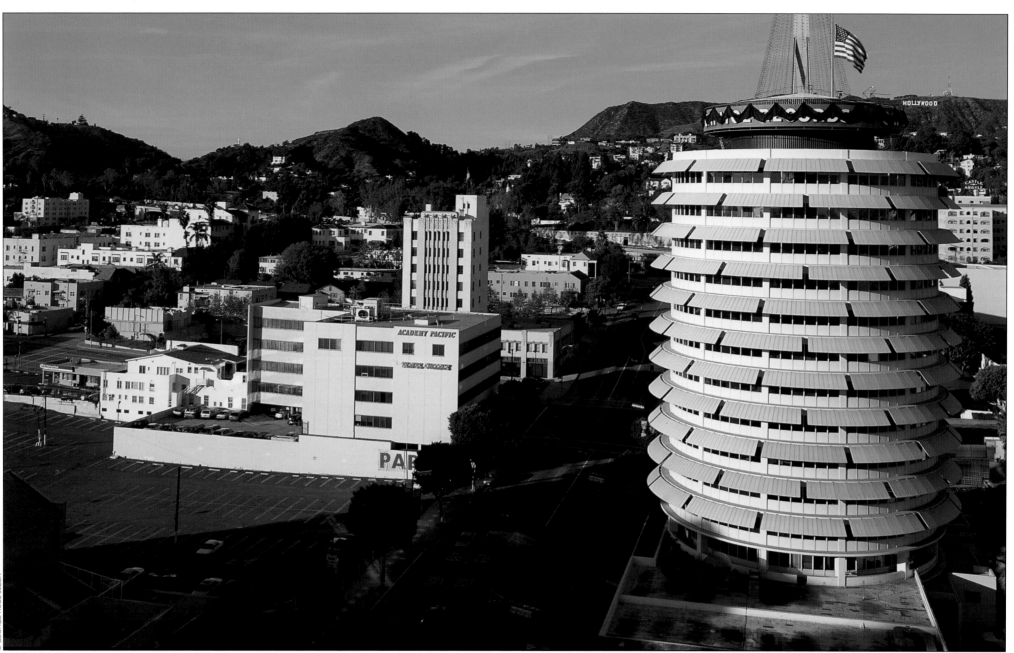

The North Vine Street skyline has changed over the years with the addition of the famous Capitol Records Building in 1956. Built by music store owner Glenn Wallichs, composer Johnny Mercer, and movie producer Buddy DeSylva, the 13-story building resembling a stack of records on a phonograph spindle was the first circular office building in the world. The 92-foot diameter building features a beacon on the roof that spells out the letters H-O-L-L-Y-W-O-O-D in Morse Code. Some of the world's greatest musicians, including Frank Sinatra, recorded in the basement recording studios. Gold record albums belonging to many of Capitol's artists are displayed in the lobby, defining the history of the company.

In 1901, the Los Angeles Pacific Boulevard and Development Company was incorporated by investors Harrison Gray Otis, publisher of the *Los Angeles Times*, Hollywood developer H.J. Whitley and builder George W. Hoover. After purchasing a tract of land on Prospect Avenue at what is now between La Brea and Highland Avenue, plans were made for Hoover to build a new hotel named the Hollywood Hotel at the northwest corner of Prospect and Highland Avenues. In February of 1903 the first 40-room unit of the hotel was completed with construction of an additional 104 rooms continuing over the next three years. The hotel register boasted many famed film stars over the years, including Douglas Fairbanks, Lon Chaney, Pola Negri, Norma Shearer, Rudolph Valentino and countless others. During the 1930s the hotel became a national shrine when Hollywood columnist Louella Parsons broadcast her radio show from the hotel.

The reputation of the Hollywood Hotel grew internationally when a major motion picture entitled *Hollywood Hotel* was made starring Dick Powell in 1937. During WWII, many service men visiting Hollywood stayed at the hotel. After the War the hotel remained a landmark until it was demolished in 1956 to make way for a bank building. With the coming of the 1960s, most of Hollywood's historic past was gone with just a few landmarks left to remind the tourists of Hollywood's past. But, it wasn't until the 1990s that the plans for a comprehensive development became a reality with the new Hollywood and Highland project, which opened in February 2002 with interior design taken from the famous 1916 D.W. Girffith film *Intolerence.*

Early Hollywood, as seen from the intersection of Highland and Franklin Avenues, was a real estate developer's dream. On the left, the Hollywood Hotel is seen under construction, at the corner of Prospect and Highland Avenues. This tract was purchased in 1901, beginning a development that would last for the next one hundred years. It was in these open fields that a city was born, a place that grew into one of the most famous locales in the world.

The area around Highland and Franklin grew slowly over the years with the construction of major landmarks. As seen in this photograph from Whitley Heights, the development had been steady, with significant structures built throughout Hollywood's first century. The First Methodist Church (seen on the right) was built in 1930, and the dramatic Hollywood Renaissance Hotel on Highland was completed in 2002.

Hollywoodland Realty built the Hollywood Sign high on Mount Lee to advertise the development of Hollywoodland Estates. Harry Chandler of the *Los Angeles Times* suggested that the company create a large sign reading *Hollywoodland* on the hillside above the development. The suggestion turned out to be one of the world's longest lasting marketing plans.

The sign consisted of thirteen letters 50-feet high, 30-feet wide made of sheet metal, pipe, wire, telephone poles and hundreds of 40-watt bulbs.

The construction cost was $21,000. As seen in this photo, Hollywoodland was dedicated by

developer S. H. Woodruff and his company employees in 1923.

BRUCE TORRENCE HISTORICAL COLLECTION

In 1949, the Hollywood Chamber of Commerce restored the sign after years of neglect and removed the word "LAND," leaving the name HOLLYWOOD. The sign suffered further deterioration and was restored in 1978. The public came to its rescue with donations to rebuild the icon at a cost of $27,000 per letter, more than the cost of the entire original sign.

After the Hollywoodland real estate office and entrance gates were built at 2700 North Beachwood Drive, the sales force was put to work immediately. S. H. Woodruff, the developer of the project, planned a sales campaign that was as grand as the promotion of a Hollywood motion picture. Having lured such film notables as comedy producer Mack Sennett into investing in property, publicity of this event alone would ensure the project's success. The most expensive lot sold for $55,000 and the least for $2,500. The area in front of the real estate office was zoned for commercial building.

The entrance gates to Hollywoodland remind visitors that they are entering a historic zone. Most of the original lots offered during the 1920s were developed, but the rapid growth of Hollywoodland was hindered and delayed by the Depression of the 1930s. During that time most construction was frozen but sales picked up after World War II, growing steadily into the 1960s.

Looking west to Rockcliff Drive from Deronda, the Hollywoodland development takes shape with Castillo Del Lago in the background on the ridge to the left. In 1923 Harry Chandler, publisher of the *Los Angeles Times*, and M. H. Sherman, director of the Pacific Electric Railway Company, brought the developers to the canyon. Chandler and Sherman formed a key syndicate in the real estate boom across Los Angeles headed by S. H. Woodruff, who with his partner, Tracy E. Shoults and a team of salesmen made Hollywoodland a reality.

DINO AND GREG WILLIAMS COLLECTION

Today Hollywoodland has been fully developed with the Hollywoodland Real Estate Company continuing to sell properties in a re-energized market. The popularity of old Hollywood style homes coupled with the close proximity to both downtown Hollywood and Los Angeles, continues to make the Hollywoodland district a choice place to live.

Hollywoodland at this time consisted of thousands of acres that were divided into home sites, with views of Hollywood below.
At this time prominent architects of the day were called in to construct the houses, many of which were in the
Spanish or Italian Romanesque style. Beachwood Canyon at the foot of the Hollywood hills was a
section of the Albert Beach Ranch in the early part of the 20th century.

Hollywoodland became a popular place to live in the 1920s. When well-known film industry celebrities began moving in, the area became highly desirable. The "King of Comedy" Mack Sennett, an investor in Hollywoodland, was one of the first to build a major mansion at the top of the hill. With the motion picture studios so close, many studio employees who could afford a house in the hills moved to Hollywoodland.

The Kerrigan House is located in Cahuenga Terrace, nestled in the hills at the east entrance to the Cahuenga Pass near the John Anson Ford Theater (originally known as the Pilgrimage Theater) and under the famous Hollywood cross that was put on the hill above the theater in 1923. Large and small estates were built in these neighborhoods. Many featured Spanish-Mediterranean architecture, often with classical details reminiscent of European opulence.

Hollywood's architectural eclecticism attracted businessmen, as well as show business people during the 1920s and 1930s. The prominent people who bought homes in the Hollywood Hills throughout those decades often built mini-palaces, some ornate, some whimsical. Many of these houses still exist in their original form and are now in demand by a new generation of buyers who want a piece of Hollywood history.

LOS ANGELES PUBLIC LIBRARY

In 1922 a Hollywood Dam committee was formed by the Chamber of Commerce with William Mulholland, the pioneering water engineer. Mulholland was brought in to supervise the future dam and the resultant lake, and would act as the spearhead for future development of the area's water resources. The lower part of Weid Canyon at the north end of Wilcox and Vine was to be the site of the new construction. Work was begun in August 1923 and completed in December 1924, with Dedication ceremonies that were held on March 17, 1925.

Lake Hollywood is an oasis above the bustling city, invisible to most residents in the area. The dam, unknown to most who live in or visit Hollywood, is covered with an earth-wall, foliage and stands 200 feet high. Engineers came from all over to view it, and most agreed that it was one of the most beautiful dam designs in the United States. The lake has been supplying Hollywood with most of its water for more than 75 years and continues to be one of Hollywood's most treasured assets.

Lookout Mountain, located at the top of Laurel Canyon in the west Hollywood Hills, became a popular site around the turn of the
century. Many outdoor enthusiasts would trek to the top of the mountain to see a spectacular view of Hollywood below.
In 1908 Lookout Mountain was subdivided into bungalow lots, and by 1910 Lookout Mountain Inn was
built consisting of a 24-room hotel with a pavilion and restaurant.

The view from Lookout Mountain is an unobstructed 270-degree view of Los Angeles that is worth the trip to the top of Laurel Canyon. The original inn was destroyed by fire in 1918, after that the property was developed into residential lots. During the 1960s, Laurel Canyon and its Lookout Mountain Avenue were home to many legendary rock musicians and the parties that attracted many from around the world. Singer Joni Mitchell lived in the canyon for many years and wrote many of her songs there. The area's beauty and solitude inspired her and many other people over the last one hundred years.

Edendale, a small community just north of Downtown (and now considered part of Echo Park) became home to the first permanent
motion picture studio facilities in Los Angeles beginning in 1909. The Mack Sennett/Keystone Studio was established on
Glendale Boulevard in 1912 on the site where the Bison Film Company had opened its doors in 1909. Sennett Studios
gave birth to Charles Chaplin, Roscoe Arbuckle, Mabel Normand and the Keystone Kops. It was in the Edendale hills
where the antics of the Keystone Kops and other comedic actors were filmed between 1909 and 1928.

By the 1920s, the various studios in Edendale (presently a part of the Echo Park District north of downtown Los Angeles) grew too large for the neighborhood and moved into Hollywood proper. Although the Selig Polyscope Company built the first studio in Edendale in 1909, the area was all but forgotten by filmmakers. In 1982, a plaque commemorating the Mack Sennett/Keystone Studio was placed on the original concrete-reinforced, enclosed stage. The historic structure is now owned by Public Storage, but remains an important relic of Edendale's past.

Taken from high atop Mount Lee, this photograph captures the view south to Beachwood Drive and over the Hollywood Sign (seen in the foreground). When the Hollywoodland development was first developed Beachwood Canyon and the Hollywood Hills was a rural area teeming with wildlife and a potential for catastrophic fires. But developers didn't care; the potential for big dollars was there. The development became one of the most important building booms in the Los Angeles area, with the Hollywood Sign as its enduring symbol.

This spectacular view of the Hollywood Hills with Lake Hollywood at the right, shows a sight that most Angelenos never see nor even know exists. Lake Hollywood and the Hollywood Hills are still considered "Hidden Hollywood" with locals proud of their historic neighborhood. Daily hikers, tourists and locals trek their way into the hills around Lake Hollywood to experience a little of the wilderness that once dominated the area.

The Hollywood Palladium opened its doors on October 31, 1940, four months after Lana Turner, with a silver shovel, took part in the groundbreaking ceremonies. The auditorium was a major nightlife scene in Hollywood for more than 60 years. Entertainers such as Freddie Martin and his ochestra, Tommy and Jimmy Dorsey and their bands, Judy Garland, Harry James, Betty Grable, Doris Day, Les Brown and his band, Benny Goodman, Peggy Lee, Marilyn Monroe and Glenn Miller and his band appeared on a regular basis.

The Los Angeles Times publisher Norman Chandler funded the construction of the Palladium at a cost of $1.6 million in 1940.
The popular Hollywood venue hosted U.S. Presidents, including Harry S. Truman, Dwight D. Eisenhower, John F. Kennedy,
Lyndon B. Johnson and Richard M. Nixon. In 1961 the Palladium became the television home of bandleader
Lawrence Welk, who became a fixture in America's living rooms for many years. In more recent times,
the Palladium was the stage of many rock shows, industry award shows, and conventions.

For more than 75 years, Hollywood Boulevard between Cahuenga Boulevard and Vine Street has been the traditional "downtown Hollywood," much like Times Square in New York. The Taft Building, on the left, was the first high-rise built at the intersection in 1924, followed by the Equitable Building, on the northeast corner in 1930. But the most architecturally significant was the new Pantages Theater building at Argyle Avenue which opened on June 4, 1930.

BISON ARCHIVES

The Pantages Theater was one of the most unique and beautiful theaters built in Hollywood with an architectural style dubbed Hollywood/Aztec/Deco. The theater, designed by B. Marcus Priteca for Alexander Pantages in 1930, was by far the grandest in Hollywood since the Grauman's Chinese Theater was built in 1927. Not only the grandest Deco jewel in Hollywood, the Pantages had the distinction of being one of the best Deco theaters in the world. Because its glorious design spoke to the Hollywood dream, the Pantages Theater became the site of many premieres and home to the Academy Awards ceremonies for ten years.

Mary Pickford and Douglas Fairbanks were international motion picture superstars from 1915 to 1930. In 1919, Douglas Fairbanks moved to Beverly Hills and purchased an old hunting lodge in the hills at 1143 Summit Drive. By 1920 he renovated the place, named it Pickfair and moved in with Mary Pickford, his new bride. The estate became the 'White House' of Beverly Hills, where many international dignitaries, from presidents to princes, came to visit. During the late 1930s Mary Pickford hosted a radio program from the house, and several films featured the mansion and its grounds. The 42-room home had a 100-foot swimming pool, a first in Beverly Hills, and was the site of choice for many film industry parties and weddings.

In 1936, after Mary Pickford's divorce from Douglas Fairbanks, Pickford married actor Buddy Rogers. The pair lived at Pickfair until her death in 1979. Sports entrepreneur Jerry Buss purchased the property in 1980 and 1988 sold it to singer Pia Zadora. It was demolished in 1990 to build a large Mediterranean villa on the site, where tours still drive by the site of Pickfair. Now the historic home, that once was the social center of Beverly Hills, is just a memory.

At one time the intersection of Prospect and Talmadge in East Hollywood was one of the most important studio centers in the world.
This view shows the southwest corner, including a view of director D.W. Griffith's *Intolerance* sets,
one of the largest sets ever been built in Hollywood.

Parts of east Hollywood have not changed over the years. A perfect example is the intersection of Prospect Avenue and Talmadge Street, seen here at the southwest corner, still features some of the homes in their original state. Nearby on Kingswell Avenue is the home of Walt Disney's uncle. Walt lived there and used to walk over to the old studios nearby to see the filmaking activities. It was the Prospect and Talmadge area that inspired Walt Disney to open his own studio of animation only a few blocks away.

Christie-Nestor Studio's director-general Al Christie and the "King of Comedy" Mack Sennett teamed up with developers to create Mack Sennett Studios and a new "studio city" in 1927.
The Republic Studios, seen here on the north side of Ventura Boulevard, first took over the Mack Sennett Studios in 1934 and then the Mascot Studios in 1935.
The new "city" of Studio City slowly grew until around 1932, when the Great Depression stymied further development.
It wasn't until 1946 that Studio City started to expand again with an influx of
new people coming from around the United States.

In 1935, when Republic expanded, the studio produced many westerns, serials and dramas starring Roy Rogers, Ray "Crash" Corrigan, Tex Ritter, Buster Crabbe (who starred in *Buck Rogers* and *Flash Gordon*) and many others. By the 1950s the studio property was taken over by CBS where television series such as *Gunsmoke* and later *The Mary Tyler Moore Show, The Wild Wild West, The Bob Newhart Show, St. Elsewhere, Roseanne, Hillstreet Blues,* and in the 90s, *Seinfeld* were taped. Dubbed CBS Studio Center, the lot presently located at Ventura Boulevard and Radford Avenue is still an important motion picture and television production center in the Los Angeles area where feature films such as *The Addams Family* were shot.

BISON ARCHIVES

One of the more historic studios in Hollywood is Paramount. Having moved from its original location at Sunset Boulevard and Vine Street in 1926, the company expanded the lot to become one of the largest studios in the heart of Hollywood. Founders Jesse Lasky, Cecil B. DeMille and Adolph Zukor guided the company throughout Hollywood's golden era with stars such as Gloria Swanson, Clara Bow, Gary Cooper, Marlene Dietrich and Claudette Colbert. Paramount stars appeared in such classic films as *The Ten Commandments (1923), IT (1927), Cleopatra (1934), Desire (1936), Beau Geste (1939)* and *Sunset Boulevard* (1950).

Paramount Studios, located on Melrose Avenue just east of Gower Street, is still one of the busiest motion picture companies in town, making feature films as well as television shows on its lot. The *Star Trek* television shows and feature films have dominated the lot for the past 20 years. A selection of films produced on the Paramount lot includes: *Ghost, Forrest Gump, The Hunt For Red October,* and *Clear and Present Danger.* The Paramount Studio with its signature 'Bronson Gate' endures as one of Hollywood's historic studio lots as well as a current film and television production center.

© GEORGE ROSS JEZEK

This corner of Melrose Avenue and Gower Street has been one of the most lavish Hollywood landmarks since the corner stage and RKO logo "Earth-Radio Tower" was built in 1935. There Fred Astaire and Ginger Rogers danced, King Kong beat his chest and Orson Welles filmed *Citizen Kane*. RKO Pictures took over the old F.B.O. Studios of Joseph P. Kennedy in 1928 and built on that site a modern motion picture studio. Specializing in 'sound' pictures, the company prospered. Later Howard Hughes purchased the RKO Studio property and made *The Outlaw* starring Jane Russell on the lot.

Located on the northeast corner of Melrose Avenue and Gower Street, Paramount Studios is home to the west coast headquarters of Paramount Pictures, a division of Viacom. In 1957, the old RKO lot became Desilu Studios owned by Lucille Ball and Desi Arnaz. By 1967 it was taken over entirely by Paramount and the two lots merged into one. Such television shows as *Happy Days, Taxi* and *Cheers* were made there along with many feature films. Also located on the lot is KCAL Channel 9 News, one of Southern California's most popular news stations, housed in the old *Mork and Mindy* and *Laverne and Shirley* television show stages.

In this photograph looking east along Sunset Boulevard east of Gower Street, two children can be seen walking along the muddy road lined with pepper and eucalyptus trees. After WWI, the Hollywood area went through a major transition from rural area to modern city. The roads were paved, businesses were built, city services were improved and expanded along with a growing population from around the world.

The once muddy road in the middle of fields evolved into the Sunset Boulevard of today, a thoroughfare that traverses the city from Downtown at its east end, to the Pacific at its west end. Many observers have noted that traveling from one end of Sunset to the other shows visitors the full range of life in Los Angeles: its richest to its poorest, its most flamboyant to its most serene, its ethnic diversity and its varying cultural themes. Here, at the intersection of Sunset and Wilcox Avenue, the CNN building is seen at the right, near where the old Hollywood Canteen once stood.

Just east of Fairfax Avenue, horse-drawn graders are seen working on residential subdivisions near Sunset Boulevard. The area was under constant development since 1883. What is now West Hollywood along Sunset Boulevard was part of the rural area of Hollywood until the early 1930s, when many of the residential neighborhoods were developed. People from around the United States were coming to this part of Los Angeles for affordable real estate opportunities.

© GEORGE ROSS JEZEK

Sunset Boulevard just east of Fairfax is a combination of residential areas and commercial buildings. The Directors Guild of America, motion picture and recording industry agents offices, and special restaurants have lined the famed Boulevard for decades. The intersection of Fairfax and Sunset Boulevard has been the unofficial beginning of the Sunset Strip that ends to the west at Doheny Drive.

The Sunset Towers, built in 1930, was the first high-rise apartment house on the Strip. The area was part of a then unincorporated section of Los Angeles that is now West Hollywood. The Sunset Towers, with its Art Deco architecture, was recognized as Hollywood's most elegant place to live. During the 1930s Harry Culver, the developer of Culver City, lived in the Sunset Towers after having lost most of his fortune during the depression era years.

The old Sunset Towers became a hotel and is today now known as the Argyle, a trendy Sunset Strip hangout. The old restaurants and clubs of the past have been transformed into new favorites, all proof positive that the Strip is the root of social trends, a big draw for both trendsetters and followers. The Argyle, with its spectacular views of Los Angeles, is a popular historic site which continually hosts industry parties and guests as it always has for over seventy years.

The first high-rise building at the intersection of Hollywood Boulevard and Vine was opened in 1924. It housed offices for motion picture industry executives as well as dentists, accountants, lawyers and other business people. The Taft brothers, relatives of President Taft, razed the Hollywood Memorial Church that stood on the site in 1923 and built the 12-story Taft Building in 65 days. Its 1924 opening drew motion picture stars and boxer Jack Dempsey who made a special appearance.

The Taft Building is one of the remarkable landmarks at the southeast corner of Hollywood and Vine, an authentic relic of old Hollywood. It continues to house a diverse group of businesses, many of which are still motion picture industry related. The historic building is one of Hollywood's most treasured sites that was the center of downtown Hollywood's cultural and economic life for over eighty years.

BISON ARCHIVES

Universal City was established as a motion picture studio on the Taylor Horse Ranch in the North Hollywood township in 1912. By 1913, the studio became a municipality (under North Hollywood) known as Universal City, complete with its own mayor and city officials elected by the stars and executives. The studio itself was designed in the Spanish-Mission style, fronting Lankershim Boulevard and was completed in 1915. Shortly thereafter, tours of the studio and its production facilities were offered. A Mecca for silent stars, Universal was home to Lon Chaney and Mary Philbin in *The Phantom of the Opera* (1925) and Lew Ayres of *All Quiet At The Western Front* (1930). With the coming of sound films in the early 1930s, new Universal stars and productions made Universal an international success. The studio was rebuilt with modern sound stages and new facilities. Motion pictures such as *Frankenstein*, *Dracula*, musicals starring Deanna Durbin and comedies starring Abbott and Costello made Universal Studios one of the world's major studios.

No longer just a film studio, today Universal City is a world-class amusement park hosting millions of tourists and locals. In addition to the studio tour, which features thrill rides based on Universal films, the facility also features Universal City Walk, a shopping and theater complex designed by renowned Southern California architect John Jerde. Universal has been taken over by several major international media firms over the years, but the motion picture and television operations along with its tours and attractions continue to keep the old studio lot a major economic asset to the area.

Selma Avenue and Vine Street was one of the most important corners in Hollywood when the southeast corner was occupied by the Lasky Feature Play Company which later became Paramount Pictures. Established at Selma and Vine in the Stern Family horse barn, remodeled as a studio and laboratory building, the first Hollywood feature film, *The Squaw Man,* was made there in 1914. The Lasky-DeMille Barn is now the Hollywood Heritage Museum across from the Hollywood Bowl. In the 1930s, North Vine Street was the heart of nightlife in Hollywood with its famous theaters and restaurants all within a block of each other. On the east side of Vine was the Hollywood Brown Derby, one of Hollywood's legendary historic sites that was demolished in 1994.

North Vine Street just south of Hollywood Boulevard is in the process of change. Many of its historic landmarks are gone, such as the Brown Derby, Mike Lyman's Cafe, the Hollywood Rooftop Ballroom, Hollywood Bowling, Ah Fongs Restaurant and the Merv Griffin Theater. The intersection of Hollywood and Vine has gone under several renovations and the immediate area around Vine is continuing to be developed and improved. New businesses are opening and new people are coming to Hollywood. The old Huntington Hartford Theater now owned by Nosotros (Latin theater group) is again a gathering place for live theater productions and the old Hollywood Entertainment complex on the west side of Vine Street at this time is in the process of redevelopment.

One of the early Hollywood studios, Vitagraph of America, originally established in New York before the turn of the 20th century, arrived in Santa Monica in 1911 and then moved to East Hollywood by 1915. Located on the northeast corner of Prospect Avenue and Talmadge Street, the studio made many films on the site starring such celebrities as Anita Stewart, Larry Semon, Antonio Moreno, Norma and Constance Talmadge among many others. In 1925 Warner Bros. Pictures purchased the Vitagraph Company assets and the lot was re-named the Warner-Vitagraph studio where many Warner pictures were made such as *The Sea Beast* (1926), *The Jazz Singer* (1927), and later *Captain Blood* (1935).

Throughout the 1920s and 1950s Warner Bros. operated the East Hollywood studio making shorts and features there. Other companies took advantage of the facilities as well, because of the wide assortment of back lot settings. By 1948, ABC purchased the lot, renaming it ABC Television Center, and immediately converted the facilities into television studios. By September 16, 1949, the gates were opened to what was then the world's largest television plant, housing studios and general administrative headquarters for ABC on the Pacific coast. The KECA call letters were changed to KABC in 1953 and are still in use today.

At the northeast corner of Hollywood Boulevard and Wilcox Avenue stands the Warner Hollywood Theater building with its signature twin radio towers on either end of its roofline. The theater was built in 1927 on the site of famed painter Paul DeLongpre's estate on Hollywood Boulevard. Although the theater was originally designated to open Warner's first commercial sound picture, *The Jazz Singer*, Sam Warner died suddenly and the new theater was closed. It opened a year later with *The Glorious Betsy*. Designed by architect G. Albert Landsburgh, the theater's exterior architecture is in the Italian Renaissance style, and the interior follows the Spanish-Moorish theme that was popular on Hollywood Boulevard at the height of the 1920s.

When the Warner Theater opened in 1928, KFWB radio was transferred there from Warner Bros. Studios on Sunset Boulevard. By 1929 the two broadcasting towers were constructed at each end of the roof overlooking the Boulevard. In 1968 Pacific Theatres purchased the old Warner Theater, where it still stands as one of Hollywood's most precious landmarks. The double towers were lit with blue neon in the late 1990s.

One of the most historic Hollywood studios still existing is the Warner Bros. Studio at Sunset and Van Ness. Established there in an empty field in 1920, Warner Studios in Hollywood brought the public such films as *Rin Tin Tin*, John Barrymore in *Don Juan*, Al Jolson in *The Jazz Singer* and later became the home of the animation unit featuring Bugs Bunny and Daffy Duck. Warner was the first to employ the Vitaphone, which revolutionized the motion picture industry. The technical headquarters of Vitaphone were located nearby at the corner of DeLongpre and Van Ness Avenue and by the 1930s, the offices became the animation department for Warner Bros.

In 1955, Paramount's KTLA television division was moved to the old Warner lot, but by 1964 it was sold to Golden West Broadcasting which was owned by western star Gene Autry. In more recent times the lot changed hands again, with the studio becoming the Tribune Hollywood Studios, a Chicago-based company. The studio now is a rental lot serving the Hollywood production community with commercials, television shows and features produced there. Many of the original buildings, including the Mount Vernon look-alike administration building, still stand.

In 1901 when the Los Angeles Pacific Boulevard and Development Company was born, land was purchased north of Hollywood Boulevard and sections of it were split among the partners for development. The property north of Franklin Avenue was given to H. J. Whitley who developed his Whitley Heights, a residential tract. From the 1920s on, Hollywood legends such as Rudolph Valentino and Janet Gaynor lived in the Heights. Architectural styles were diverse in the Heights: Spanish, Mediterranean, Tudor, and Spanish-Colonial houses stood side by side, perhaps a reflection of the cultural diversity of Los Angeles itself.

When the Hollywood Freeway was built, it bisected Whitley Heights, and in the process the Rudolph Valentino house was lost. Today the old Whitley Heights continues to be a Hollywood historic district with its old homes overlooking a changing Hollywood of the present, but reflecting a Hollywood of the past. Now recognized as a trendy place to live, Whitley Heights is home to a new generation of young entrepreneurs and people of the entertainment industry.

In 1915 an old farm at the southwest corner of Sunset Boulevard and Western Avenue was transformed into a movie studio by Thomas Dixon who wrote the famed novel, *The Clansman* (that same year, film director D.W. Griffith translated it into *The Birth of a Nation*). By 1916, when the William Fox Company came to Hollywood, it settled into the Dixon Studio, where Fox produced many films of the silent era. In the 1940s, the studio became 20th Century-Fox Television while the feature films continued to be produced at the 20th Century Fox lot in what is now Century City.

© GEORGE ROSS JEZEK

This photograph focusing northeast on Western Avenue at Sunset Boulevard captures the longtime site of the William Fox Studios in Hollywood, home to the silent films of Tom Mix, Theda Bara, George O'Brien and Buck Jones. In 1971 the studio gave way to commercial development, leaving only the Fox laboratory at Fernwood Avenue, which is still in operation. The Deluxe Color laboratory (still owned by Fox) is one of last vestiges of historic Hollywood in this neighborhood.

The publisher would like to thank the following individuals and organizations who helped make this book possible.

George M. Jezek, Sr.

Mr. Johnny Grant

Marc Wanamaker

Ronda Millward

Justin Mink

John and Lois Jesek

Suzanne and Steve Arriaga

John Grondona and Family

Zach A. Johnson

Bruce Torrence

Dino and Greg Williams

Jackie Lugo

Los Angeles Public Library

Bison Archives

Carolyn Cole

Fuji Film USA

Team Reprographics

Tamara and Ashlyn Jimenez

Eva Grandison and Family

Wahrenbrocks Book House

Chuck Valverde

Jan Tonnesen

Mike Boyd

Johnny Navarro

Robert Harrington

Chrome Film and Digital

Dennis Reiter

Hollywood at Vine

Sheila Holincheck

Roosevelt Hotel

Hollywood Chamber of Commerce

Hyatt Regency, West Hollywood

The Riboli Family

L.A.P.D.

God and Country

I would like to acknowledge the help and support of a lifelong friend who recently passed away. Stephen (Reno) Hartley helped me with many of my photographic assignments throughout the years. You were a great friend that I could always count on. Reno you will be missed by all.

George Ross Jezek

(Next Page)

CBS • Columbia Square

The Christie Film Company, which took over the old Nestor studio at Gower Street and Sunset Boulevard in 1916, later became a rental studio and in 1937 was sold to the Columbia Broadcasting Corporation. In 1938, Columbia Square was built to house the KNX West Coast flagship station in Hollywood. Today Columbia Square is the headquarters of CBS News operations.

Photography: © George Ross Jezek